RECON MARINES

by Edward Voeller

Consultant:
Major G.F. Marte, USMC, Ret.
Executive Director
Force Recon Association

CAPSTONE BOOKS

an imprint of Capstone Press
Mankato, Minnesota

Capstone Books are published by Capstone Press
151 Good Counsel Drive, P.O. Box 669, Mankato, Minnesota 56002
http://www.capstone-press.com

Library of Congress Cataloging-in-Publication Data
Voeller, Edward A.
  U.S. Marine Corps special forces: Recon Marines/by Edward Voeller.
  p.cm.—(Warfare and weapons)
  Includes bibliographical references and index.
  Summary: Introduces the Marine Corps special forces known as the Recon
Marines, describing their mission, history, and the equipment they use.
  ISBN 0-7368-0339-4
  1. United States. Marine Corps—Juvenile literature. 2. Special forces (Military
science)—United States—Juvenile literature. 3. Scouts and scouting—United States
Juvenile literature. [1. United States. Marine Corps. 2. Special forces (Military
science)]. I. Title. II. Title: US Marine Corps special forces. III. Series.
VE23.V63 2000
359.9'6413—dc21

99-21031
CIP

Editorial Credits
Connie R. Colwell, editor; Timothy Halldin, cover designer; Linda Clavel,
  illustrator; Heidi Schoof, photo researcher

Photo Credits
Archive Photos, 10, 13, 15
David Bohrer, cover, 4, 7, 18, 22, 28, 31, 33, 36, 39, 45
Department of Defense, 20, 26, 40

**Special thanks to David Bohrer, Pulitzer Prize-winning photographer for the
Los Angeles Times, for providing the cover and interior photos.**

Table of Contents

Chapter 1

The Recon Marines

In 1965, U.S. soldiers were trying to reach the Phu Bai air base in South Vietnam by boat. At the time, the United States was helping South Vietnam fight against North Vietnam. This war was called the Vietnam War (1954–1975).

A specially trained group of soldiers patrolled beaches near the Phu Bai base. The soldiers looked for the safest route to Phu Bai. The soldiers found that the water near the beaches was too shallow for military boats.

These specially trained soldiers then patrolled the nearby Hue River. They decided this river was the safest route to Phu Bai. The other soldiers traveled to Phu Bai by the Hue River. They reached the air base safely.

Recon marines are specially trained members of the U.S. Marine Corps.

Recon Marines

The specially trained soldiers were recon marines. Recon marines are specially trained members of the U.S. Marine Corps. The Marine Corps is an amphibious force. It operates both in and out of water. Marines use ships to travel to battle sites. They then go ashore to perform their duties.

The U.S. Navy, U.S. Army, and U.S. Air Force make up the armed forces. The Marine Corps is the smallest part of the armed forces. Only 12 percent of the people serving in the armed forces are marines.

Reconnaissance

Recon marines perform many of the same duties as other members of the Marine Corps. These duties are called missions. But recon marines also have special training in reconnaissance (ree-CAH-nuh-suhns). Recon marines explore enemy territory to gain information. The United States then uses this information to prepare for battles.

Recon marines may gain many types of information about enemy forces. They may find the location of enemy troops and bases.

Recon marines learn about enemy forces by patrolling.

They may learn which weapons enemy forces carry. They may find safe landing places for other soliders to come ashore by ship or helicopter.

Recon marines rarely attack enemy forces. They work in small teams with few weapons. Recon marines try to learn about enemy forces without using their weapons.

Recon Patrol

Recon marines learn about enemy forces by patrolling. They often patrol enemy territory at

7

night. This way, enemy forces cannot see them easily. They hide themselves near enemy territory. They wear camouflage clothing and paint their skin with camouflage makeup sticks. Camouflage usually is brown, black, and dark green. These colors help recon marines blend in with their surroundings.

Recon marines move quietly through enemy territory. They watch enemy soldiers. Recon marines remain quiet for four or five days. Noise can endanger the lives of the recon marines. Recon marines communicate only with arm and hand signals and whispers.

Recon marines gather different types of information while on patrol. One team might patrol to learn the depth of a body of water. Another team might locate enemy troops.

Recon marines send this information to the Marine Corps headquarters. They often communicate with headquarters by radio. This allows them to communicate quietly.

Recon marines return to their bases after patrol. Recon marines tell their leaders what information they gained on patrol. They report everything they learned about enemy forces. Military leaders then can make battle plans.

Parachute: stands for the parachutes recon marines use to jump into enemy territory

Wings: stand for the aircraft some recon marines use to reach mission sites

Chapter 2

History of Recon Marines

Marines fought many important battles throughout the history of the United States. Marines first fought in the Revolutionary War (1775–1783). Reconnaissance was important for the early marines. Marines traveled into enemy territory during early battles to collect information. But these marines were not specially trained members of reconnaissance teams.

The First Recon Marines
After World War I (1914–1918), the Marine Corps began to train marines for reconnaissance. These specially trained

The Marine Corps fought many important battles throughout history.

marines began to perform missions in 1938. But the Marine Corps still did not have a special reconnaissance unit.

Armed forces leaders during World War II (1939–1945) needed a special unit of soldiers. These soldiers would help plan boat landings on enemy beaches. The military leaders selected marines to form the Observer Group in 1942. This was the first special reconnaissance unit. In 1943, the Observer Group became the Amphibious Reconnaissance Company.

The reconnaissance unit took part in many World War II battles. Recon marines often landed on island beaches at night. They made sure it was safe for other marines to land their boats on these beaches.

The Vietnam War

The Vietnam War was difficult for recon marines. Enemy forces in this war used guerrilla warfare. Guerrilla fighters move very fast and often change positions. It was very

Early recon marines were not specially trained members of reconnaissance teams.

difficult for recon marines to find the enemy troops. Recon marines had to act quickly. They sometimes needed helicopters to pick them up when enemy troops appeared.

Other Efforts
Recon marines have aided in other efforts since the Vietnam War. Recon marines and other special forces helped drive Iraqi forces out of the country of Kuwait during the Gulf War (1991).

In the mid-1990s, recon marines also helped provide security for the U.S. military in Somalia. The U.S. military traveled into this country to attempt to restore peace.

Recon Marines Today
Today's recon marine units are similar to the units in World War II. But today's recon marines have more special equipment, radios, and weapons to help them perform their duties.

Today's recon marines work during peacetime. These marines train, exercise, and prepare for battles. They must be prepared to help in case of emergency.

Enemy forces during the Vietnam War (1954–1975) used guerrilla warfare.

Mission

Operation: Phu Bai Air Base

Mission: Marines needed to safely arrive at the Phu Bai air base in Vietnam

Reconnaissance: Recon marines patrolled beaches 25 miles (40 kilometers) south of Hue City. They also checked the Hue River and the roads to Hue City. The recon marines learned that the water near the beaches was not deep enough for landing craft. The bodies of water behind the beaches were too deep for the marine soldiers to approach by foot.

Decision: Recon marines decided that crossing the Hue River was the safest route for the soldiers. The recon marines gave this information to military leaders. The military leaders ordered the other marines to travel across the Hue River. The marines reached the airfield safely.

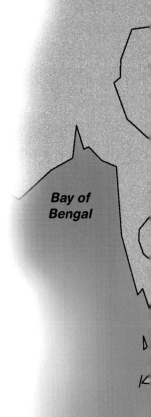

MYANMAR (BURMA)

Bay of Bengal

Chapter 3

Training

Members of the Marine Corps are volunteers. These people offer to serve in the marines. Recon marines must be members of the Marine Corps before they can be specially trained in reconnaissance. Only men can become recon marines. Congressional law does not allow women to enter ground combat specialties. These jobs may involve duties that are performed while under direct fire from enemy forces.

Boot Camp

Armed forces volunteers are called recruits. New marine recruits must attend boot camp before they can become marines. They train

---

Recon marines must be members of the Marine Corps before they can be specially trained in reconnaissance.

16 or 17 hours each day for 11 weeks at boot camp. Half of this training is in classrooms.

Boot camp training is difficult. Recruits learn the best ways to protect themselves and others. They learn how to fight in battles. They learn how to use weapons. They learn how to fight without weapons. Recruits also do a great deal of physical conditioning such as sit-ups and push-ups.

Recruits learn other survival skills at boot camp. They learn first aid. They learn to survive if their aircraft crash in water. Recruits also learn to work together and to follow orders. Marines must work in teams in order to survive during battles.

Recruits who successfully complete boot camp become marines. These marines then may volunteer for reconnaissance.

Qualifying for Reconnaissance

The Marine Corps needs experienced and well-trained marines for reconnaissance teams. Volunteers must be in top physical and mental condition.

Recon marines need special training to perform special operations.

Recon marines must be mentally qualified for their duties.

The Marine Corps tests reconnaissance volunteers to learn if they have the necessary qualities. The volunteers must pass a difficult qualifying test to enter reconnaissance training. This test is called Recon Indoctrination.

Recon Indoctrination
Recon Indoctrination starts early in the morning. Marines must first complete several exercise tests. These tests include pull-ups, sit-ups, push-ups, and a 3-mile

(5-kilometer) run. The marines then run an obstacle course. This track has many objects blocking the runners' paths. The marines must get past all the obstacles.

Marines then must complete several endurance tests. They must swim long distances in a pool. They must tread water for 30 minutes. They must swim while holding a brick out of the water. The marines also hike for 10 miles (16 kilometers) over a hilly course. During the hike, they carry a 50-pound (23-kilogram) backpack.

Recon marines also must be mentally qualified for their duties. The marines take mental tests to prove they are qualified for reconnaissance duties. These tests measure the marines' intelligence. The marines then have interviews with marine officials.

The marines can quit this qualifying test at any time. Marines who quit the qualifying test have to wait a month before retaking the test. Only about one in 10 marines passes the qualifying test. Marines who pass the test are selected to enter reconnaissance training.

Reconnaissance Training

The reconnaissance training program lasts six weeks. It includes physical training and classroom work. Recon marine volunteers learn how to gather information about the enemy forces and enemy territory.

Marines in reconnaissance training also attend two special schools. This school training lasts about two months. Marines first attend Survival, Evasion, Resistance, and Escape (SERE) school. At SERE, marines learn how to use camouflage to blend into their surroundings. They also learn the best ways to hide from enemy forces.

The marines in reconnaissance training then attend the Jungle Environment Survival Training (JEST) school. At JEST, marines learn how to find food and fresh water in the jungle. They learn which animals and plants are safe to eat.

Not all reconnaissance training schools belong to the Marine Corps. Some marines train at the army's Ranger school or Jump school. They also train with navy scuba divers. Scuba stands for "self-contained underwater breathing apparatus." Scuba divers wear tanks of compressed air when they dive into water. This allows divers to reach depths of 100 feet (30 meters) or more.

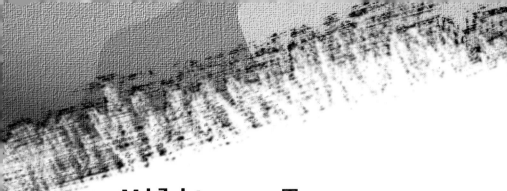

Military Terms

Cammie Stick – camouflage stick

Chopper – helicopter

Clutch – a difficult situation

Grunt – ground soldier

Harbor Site – an overnight position

JEST – Jungle Environment Survival Training

John Wayne – can opener

Light Stick – flashlight

MREs – meals ready to eat

The Sack – the bed

SERE – Survival, Evasion, Resistance, and Escape

Chapter 4

Equipment and Vehicles

Recon marines use special equipment to gather information. They must carry this equipment on their bodies when they patrol. This equipment must be lightweight. This helps recon marines to travel quickly and quietly.

Camouflage

Recon marines must blend in with their surroundings. They camouflage much of their gear. All recon marines carry camouflage makeup sticks. They paint their skin the colors of shadows and plants.

Members of the Marine Corps attempt to blend in with their surroundings.

Recon marines wear soft, floppy hats. They do not wear hard helmets like other members of the Marine Corps. Recon marines can shape these soft hats easily. Recon marines can hide in small spaces better with these hats. Recon marines often put leaves or strips of cloth on these hats for camouflage. The hats also have brims. Brims stick out from hats to protect marines from the rain and sun.

Other Equipment

Recon marines carry backpacks full of equipment. Recon marines usually carry ponchos in their backpacks. These lightweight raincoats keep the recon marines dry when it rains. Recon marines also sleep in these ponchos. They do not carry sleeping bags. Sleeping bags are too large and heavy.

Recon marines carry special lightweight food in their backpacks. This food is called meals ready to eat (MREs). Recon marines add water to MREs to eat them.

Recon marines carry backpacks full of equipment.

Recon marines share the work of carrying heavy equipment. One team member may carry the team radio. Other members of the team may carry extra batteries for the radio. Team members may exchange equipment during a patrol. This prevents recon marines from becoming overtired.

Jungle Equipment
Recon marines need other special equipment for jungle patrols. These marines often carry insect repellent. This liquid keeps away jungle insects. It also can be used to remove leeches. These worms live in wet places. They live by sucking blood from people and animals. Marines also may burn insect repellent for heat.

Recon marines carry large knives in the jungle. These knives are called k-bars. The marines may use k-bars to cut paths through jungle plants. They also may use k-bars for protection against attack.

Team members may exchange equipment during a patrol.

Weapons

Recon marines carry M-16A2 rifles. These lightweight rifles weigh about 7 pounds (3 kilograms). Recon marines can use M-16A2 rifles to shoot targets almost one-half mile (.8 kilometer) away.

Recon marines also can attach grenade launchers or scopes to their rifles. Grenade launchers shoot special bombs called grenades. Recon marines look through scopes to see their targets and aim their rifles. "Starlight" scopes help recon marines see their targets and aim their rifles in the dark.

Recon marines sometimes bring other special weapons on patrol. One team member may carry a lightweight MP-5N or M249 SAW machine gun. Others on the team may carry ammunition for this gun. The leader of a team may carry an M9 pistol.

Recon marines also may carry land mines. These bombs explode when people step on them or when vehicles travel over them. Recon marines can place land mines around their

Combat Rubber Raiding Craft are easy to hide on beaches.

resting and camping areas. The land mines protect the marines from attack.

Vehicles

The Marine Corps often uses navy ships or submarines to transport marines and their equipment. Navy ships carry small boats on board. The ships do not go near enemy territory. Enemy troops can spot these large ships. Instead, the recon marines use the small boats to travel to shore. They then hide their boats on the shore.

But recon marines sometimes use Marine Corps boats to get ashore. One of these boats is the Combat Rubber Raiding Craft (CRRC). These small rubber boats are easy to hide on beaches.

Recon marines sometimes use helicopters to travel into enemy territory. The helicopters can quickly pick up the marines when necessary. Helicopters also can transport more marines and supplies to assist the recon marines.

Marine helicopters may have long ropes attached to them. Recon marines lower these ropes to the ground. They then slide down the ropes to reach the ground.

Recon marines sometimes must travel deep into enemy territory. These marines use parachutes. These large pieces of cloth allow recon marines to jump safely from aircraft. Recon marines often wait to open their parachutes until they are near the ground. This way, the enemy does not spot the parachutes as the marines float to the ground.

Important Dates

1775 – Revolutionary War begins; marines fight many important battles.

1939 – World War II begins; marines perform reconnaissance duties, but soldiers are not part of any special reconnaissance units.

1942 – Observer Group is formed; this group was the first reconnaissance unit.

1943 – the Observer Group is renamed the Amphibious Reconnaissance Company

1954 – Vietnam War begins; recon marines have difficulty fighting guerrilla fighters.

1991 – Gulf War; recon marines assist other special operations forces in driving the Iraqi army out of Kuwait.

Chapter 5

The Future

In the future, recon marines may have many of the same duties as today's recon marines. But future recon marines may perform missions in cities and towns instead of in jungles or other remote areas.

Urban Warfare

Recon marines of the future will continue to support the Marine Corps with reconnaissance. They will gather information about countries or armies that oppose the United States.

But the recon marine patrols may be different. Enemy forces may hide in buildings instead of in forests or jungles. Recon marines may have to patrol streets and skyscrapers instead of beaches.

In the future, recon marines may perform missions in cities and towns instead of in jungles.

Recon marines also will use different gear in the future. These marines may carry maps of cities instead of maps of mountains and jungles. They may carry rope ladders in their backpacks. This equipment will help them patrol tall buildings.

New Technology

Recon marines are preparing for the future. The marines already use small computers to communicate with one another. Marines use these computers to send information to headquarters. Recon marines also can use these computers to call for support.

Another type of computer helps recon marines determine their locations. The Global Positioning System (GPS) looks like a small calculator. This device uses radio signals from satellites to locate recon marine units anywhere on Earth. Satellites are spacecraft that are sent into orbit around the Earth. Satellites often take photographs of objects in space and send them back to the Earth.

The Global Positioning System (GPS) uses radio signals from satellites to locate recon marine units.

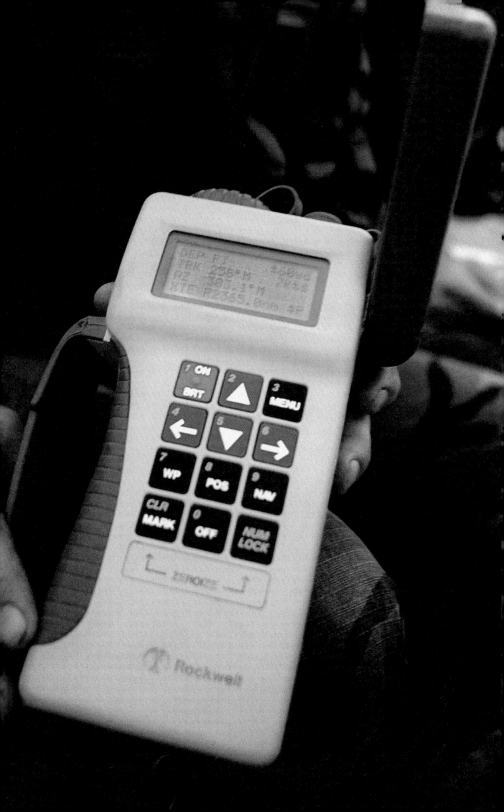

In the future, recon marines may have many of the same duties as they do today.

The Marine Corps already is using new items to help them perform their duties. Some marines wear bulletproof clothing. This clothing helps protect marines from gunshot wounds.

The Marine Corps also is developing new devices to help with its missions. The Marine Corps already operates some machines by remote control. It may use aircraft that can fly without pilots. Marines can use these vehicles to gain information from places too dangerous to patrol with soldiers. The Marine Corps also may begin to use cameras that can take photographs around corners. These cameras help recon marines stay out of danger while performing reconnaissance missions. This new technology may help recon marines serve and protect the United States.

Words to Know

amphibious (am-FI-bee-uhs)—able to work on land or water

camouflage (KA-muh-flahzh)—designs and colors that help a person or object blend in with their surroundings

grenade (gruh-NAYD)—a small weapon similar to a bomb

guerrilla (guh-RI-luh)—a fighter who moves quickly from place to place

obstacle course (OB-sti-kuhl KORS)—a running course with barriers such as walls and streams

poncho (PON-choh)—a simple nylon raincoat

reconnaissance (ree-CAH-nuh-suhns)—
exploring enemy territory to gain information

recruit (ree-KROOT)—a person in boot camp
who is trying out for the Marine Corps

urban (UR-buhn)—in a city; in the future,
recon marines will be performing duties in
urban locations.

To Learn More

Green, Michael. *The United States Marine Corps.* Serving Your Country. Mankato, Minn.: Capstone High/Low Books, 1998.

Paananen, Eloise. *The Military: Defending the Nation.* Good Citizenship. Austin, Texas: Raintree Steck-Vaughn, 1993.

Rowan, N.R. *Women in the Marines: The Boot Camp Challenge.* Minneapolis: Lerner Publications, 1994.

Warner, J.F. *The U.S. Marine Corps.* Armed Services. Minneapolis: Lerner Publications, 1991.

Useful Addresses

Force Recon Association
PMB 1775
3784-B Mission Avenue
Oceanside, CA 92054-1460

Marine Corps Air-Ground Museum
2014 Anderson Avenue
MCCDE
Quantico, VA 22134–5002

Marine Corps Division of Public Affairs
Headquarters Marine Corps
The Pentagon, Room SE–774
Washington, DC 20380-1775

Marine Corps Historical Center
Department of the Navy
9th and M Streets SE
Washington, DC 20374

Internet Sites

Force Recon Association
http://www.clearpages.com/forcerecon

United States Marine Corps
http://www.usmc.mil

Index